Book 1: Computer Science

Introduction 1.0

This Scientific Material is compiled by Michael Coffey.

Scientific Materials 1.1

Scientific Materials are materials that contain basic scientific information necessary to conduct research, understand a subject.

The paper before you is a Scientific Material.

Science 2.1

Science is the use of observation to make conclusions.

Mathematics 2.2

Mathematics is the study of logical structures.

Physics 2.3

Physics is the study of real structures.

Chemistry 2.4

Chemistry is the study of molecular structures.

Biology 2.5

Biology is the study of life.

Computer Science 2.6

Computer Science is the study of computation.

Engineering 2.7

Engineering is the use of science to create technology.

Electrical Engineering 2.8

Electrical Engineering is the purposeful use of science to create electrical technology. Electrical Engineering is a derivative of Physics, Mathematics.

Computer Engineering 2.9

Computer Engineering is the purposeful use of science to create computer technology. Computer Engineering is a derivative of Electrical Engineering, Computer Science.

Lumped Circuit Model 3.1

For a circuit, separate the discrete elements and connect them via ideal wires.

Transistor 3.2

The building blocks of logic are called transistors.

The mechanism of action differs from transistor to transistor.

Examples include Metal Oxide Semiconductor Field Effect Transistor, Bipolar Junction Transistor, Effector. This material will discuss the Effector.

Effector

Effectors receive electrons, produce electromagnetic fields as a function of receiving electrons, emit electrons from a power source.

The Effector has two terminals and like other transistors can be used to create logic gates.

Amplifier, Dampener 3.3

The Amplifier amplifies signals with external energy.

The Dampener dampens signals by diverting signal energy.

Amplifiers and dampeners adjust the signal strength with a signal degradation.

Signal degradation destroys signal information (data); this is rectified via digitalization.

Electromagnetic Circuit Model 3.4

Create a magnetic field as a function of the Effectors: $M = M_1 + M_2 + \ldots$
Create an electric field at a point: $E = f(M, x, y, z)$
The magnetic field is the flow of magnetons at the point.
The electric field is the flow of electrons at the point.

We can see how the Effector is a transistor by 'turning off' an Effector, say Effector 2 (M_2). By turning off Effector 2 (M_2), we 'affect' the electric field of the electromagnetic circuit. As another example, the effect of turning off Effector 2 (M_2) alters the electron flow such that electrons that would previously hit Effector 3 (M_3) no longer hit Effector 3, causing Effector 3 (M_3) to turn off, setting a chain reaction.

The logic gates NAND and NOR are derivable from the Electromagnetic Circuit Model equations via the use of Effectors that receive electrons, produce magnetic fields as a function of receiving electrons, emit electrons. In the following cases, the electrons emitted from the first Effector are ignored.

Let's create a NAND gate. We have an electric field that feeds two electrons to two Effectors, generating a stable magnetic field which allows for the electric field from the second Effector to feed into thin air, that is, not the third Effector.

By blocking or altering the electron from entering the first or second Effector, the magnetic field is altered such that the electric field no longer allows for the electric field from the second Effector to feed into thin air, and it now feeds into third Effector.

Therefore, we have a NAND gate.

Let's create a NOR gate. We have an electric field that feeds two electrons to two Effectors, generating a stable magnetic field which allows for the electric field from the second Effector to feed into thin air, that is, not the third Effector.

For a NOR gate, removing one electron input to either Effector one or two does not significantly affect the output magnetic and electric field from its initial state, that is, the electric field from the second Effector will feed into thin air, not the third Effector.

If both electron inputs are removed and no electrons feed into Effectors one and two, Effectors one and two will turn off such that the electric field from Effector two will feed into the third Effector.

Therefore, we have a NOR gate.

Logic Gates 4.1

NAND and NOR gates are required to architect a computer system.
NOT, AND, OR, XOR gates are derivable from NAND and NOR gates.

Boolean Algebra is used to manipulate logical equations.

Data Structures 4.2

Mathematical structures that hold data are called data structures.

They are abstractly defined in dimensions, can be visualized, and can be defined in terms of computer architecture.

Algorithms 4.3

Mathematical structures that operate data are called algorithms.

They are abstractly defined in dimensions, can be visualized, and can be defined in terms of computer architecture.

Computational Complexity Theory 4.4

Algorithms and data structures accerate in complexity. This acceration is studied in Computational Complexity Theory.

Computer Architecture System 5.1

A computer architecture system is an underlying architecture for the architecture.

Computer architecture systems provide the application programming interfaces necessary to create operating systems.

Computer architecture systems are designed with logic and application programming interfaces.

Digital Design 6.1

Verilog is used to define input and output conditions and software creates the matching algorithm.

Application Programming 7.1

Programming uses logic and application programing interfaces to create programs: logical systems designed to accomplish a purpose.

Logic is typically defined in the form of data structures and algorithms.

Application programming interfaces link to the program to the operating system.

Application Programming Interface 7.2

An application programming interface consists of an input system and an output system.

Instructions are input and feedback is recorded via output.

The feedback is read to the user, used to alter the input.

Programming Languages 7.3

Programming languages abstract logic into linguistic form.

Operating System 8.1

An operating system is an underlying architecture for the architecture.

Operating systems provide the application programming interfaces necessary to create applications.

Operating systems are designed with logic and application programming interfaces.

Book 2: Computer Engineering

Introduction 1.0

This Scientific Material is compiled by Michael Coffey.

Scientific Materials 1.1

Scientific Materials are materials that contain basic scientific information necessary to conduct research, understand a subject.

The paper before you is a Scientific Material.

Engineering 2.1

Engineering is the use of science to create technology.

Mechanical Engineering 2.2

Mechanical Engineering is the purposeful use of science to create mechanistic technology. Mechanical Engineering is a derivative of Physics, Mathematics.

Electrical Engineering 2.3

Electrical Engineering is the purposeful use of science to create electrical technology. Electrical Engineering is a derivative of Physics, Mathematics.

Aerospace Engineering 2.4

Aerospace Engineering is the purposeful use of science to create aviation technology. Aerospace Engineering is a derivative of Mechanical Engineering, Electrical Engineering.

Chemical Engineering 2.5

Chemical Engineering is the purposeful use of science to create chemical technology. Chemical Engineering is a derivative of Chemistry, Physics, Mathematics.

Computer Engineering 2.6

Computer Engineering is the purposeful use of science to create computer technology. Computer Engineering is a derivative of Electrical Engineering, Computer Science.

Material Engineering 2.7

Material Engineering is the purposeful use of science to create material technology. Material Engineering is a derivative of Chemical Engineering, Mechanical Engineering.

Biological Engineering 2.8

Biological Engineering is the purposeful use of science to create biological technology. Biological Engineering is a derivative of Computer Engineering, Biology.

Lumped Circuit Model 3.1

For a circuit, separate the discrete elements and connect them via ideal wires.

Transistor 3.2

The building blocks of logic are called transistors.
The mechanism of action differs from transistor to transistor. Examples include Metal Oxide Semiconductor Field Effect Transistor, Bipolar Junction Transistor, Effector. This material will discuss the Effector.

Effector

Effectors receive electrons, produce electromagnetic fields as a function of receiving electrons, emit electrons from a power source. The Effector has two terminals and like other transistors can be used to create logic gates.

Capacitor 3.3

The capacitor is a battery.

The capacitor is in the domain of Chemical Engineering.

The capacitor is not within the domain of Electrical Engineering.

Amplifier, Dampener 3.4

The Amplifier amplifies signals with external energy.

The Dampener dampens signals by diverting signal energy.

Amplifiers and dampeners adjust the signal strength with a signal degradation.

Signal degradation destroys signal information (data); this is rectified via digitalization.

Inductor 3.5

Inductors are solenoids that produce magnetic fields as a function of energy passthrough. The right hand rule can gauge the magnetic field output. Inductors are similar to but not the same as Effectors.

Electromagnetic Circuit Model 3.6

Create a magnetic field as a function of the Effectors: $M = M_1 + M_2 + ...$
Create an electric field at a point: $E = f(M, x, y, z)$
The magnetic field is the flow of magnetons at the point.
The electric field is the flow of electrons at the point.

We can see how the Effector is a transistor by 'turning off' an Effector, say Effector 2 (M_2). By turning off Effector 2 (M_2), we 'affect' the electric field of the electromagnetic circuit. As another example, the effect of turning off Effector 2 (M_2) alters the electron flow such that electrons that would previously hit Effector 3 (M_3) no longer hit Effector 3, causing Effector 3 (M_3) to turn off, setting a chain reaction.

The logic gates NAND and NOR are derivable from the Electromagnetic Circuit Model equations via the use of Effectors that receive electrons, produce magnetic fields as a function of receiving electrons, emit electrons. In the following cases, the electrons emitted from the first Effector are ignored.

Let's create a NAND gate. We have an electric field that feeds two electrons to two Effectors, generating a stable magnetic field which allows for the electric field from the second Effector to feed into thin air, that is, not the third Effector.

By blocking or altering the electron from entering the first or second Effector, the magnetic field is altered such that the electric field no longer allows for the electric field from the second Effector to feed into thin air, and it now feeds into the third Effector.

Therefore, we have a NAND gate.

Let's create a NOR gate. We have an electric field that feeds two electrons to two Effectors, generating a stable magnetic field which allows for the electric field from the second Effector to feed into thin air, that is, not the third Effector.

For a NOR gate, removing one electron input to either Effector one or two does not significantly affect the output magnetic and electric field from its initial state, that is, the electric field from the second Effector will feed into thin air, not the third Effector.

If both electron inputs are removed and no electrons feed into Effectors one and two, Effectors one and two will turn off such that the electric field from Effector two will feed into the third Effector.

Therefore, we have a NOR gate.

Logic Gates 4.1

NAND and NOR gates are required to architect a computer system. NOT, AND, OR, XOR gates are derivable from NAND and NOR gates.

Boolean Algebra is used to manipulate logical equations.

Data Structures 4.2

Mathematical structures that hold data are called data structures.

They are abstractly defined in dimensions, can be visualized, and can be defined in terms of computer architecture.

Algorithms 4.3

Mathematical structures that operate data are called algorithms.

They are abstractly defined in dimensions, can be visualized, and can be defined in terms of computer architecture.

Computer Architecture System 5.1

A computer architecture system is an underlying architecture for the architecture.

Computer architecture systems provide the application programming interfaces necessary to create operating systems.

Computer architecture systems are designed with logic and application programming interfaces.

Digital Design 6.1

Verilog is used to define input and output conditions and software creates the matching algorithm.

Synthesis 6.2

The synthesis of circuits is in the field of Chemical Engineering.

Application Programming 7.1

Programming uses logic and application programing interfaces to create programs: logical systems designed to accomplish a purpose.

Logic is typically defined in the form of data structures and algorithms.

Application programming interfaces link to the program to the operating system.

Application Programming Interface 7.2

An application programming interface consists of an input system and an output system.
Instructions are input and feedback is recorded via output.

The feedback is read to the user, used to alter the input.

Programming Languages 7.3

Programming languages abstract logic into linguistic form.

Operating System 8.1

An operating system is an underlying architecture for the architecture.

Operating systems provide the application programming interfaces necessary to create applications.
Operating systems are designed with logic and application programming interfaces.

Positronic Fields 9.1

Derive a positronic field:
$P = f(M, x, y, z)$
The positronic field represents the flow of positrons at the point.

The positronic field is the inverse of the electric field:
$E = f(M, x, y, z)$ so $P = g(E, x, y, z) = g(f(M, x, y, z), x, y, z)$

Book 3: Biological Engineering

Introduction 1.0

This Scientific Material is compiled by Michael Coffey.

Scientific Materials 1.1

Scientific Materials are materials that contain basic scientific information necessary to conduct research, understand a subject.

The paper before you is a Scientific Material.

Science 2.1

Science is the use of observation to make conclusions.

Mathematics 2.2

Mathematics is the study of logical structures.

Physics 2.3

Physics is the study of real structures.

Chemistry 2.4

Chemistry is the study of molecular structures.

Biology 2.5

Biology is the study of life.

Computer Science 2.6

Computer Science is the study of computation.

Engineering 3.0

Engineering is the use of science to create technology.

Mechanical Engineering 3.1

Mechanical Engineering is the purposeful use of science to create mechanistic technology. Mechanical Engineering is a derivative of Physics, Mathematics.

Electrical Engineering 3.2

Electrical Engineering is the purposeful use of science to create electrical technology. Electrical Engineering is a derivative of Physics, Mathematics.

Aerospace Engineering 3.3

Aerospace Engineering is the purposeful use of science to create aviation technology. Aerospace Engineering is a derivative of Mechanical Engineering, Electrical Engineering.

Chemical Engineering 3.4

Chemical Engineering is the purposeful use of science to create chemical technology. Chemical Engineering is a derivative of Chemistry, Physics, Mathematics.

Computer Engineering 3.5

Computer Engineering is the purposeful use of science to create computer technology. Computer Engineering is a derivative of Electrical Engineering, Computer Science.

Material Engineering 3.6

Material Engineering is the purposeful use of science to create material technology. Material Engineering is a derivative of Chemical Engineering, Mechanical Engineering.

Biological Engineering 3.7

Biological Engineering is the purposeful use of science to create biological technology. Biological Engineering is a derivative of Computer Engineering, Biology.

Molecular Biology 4.0

Molecular Biology is the study of molecular structures in biology. It is sometimes known as Micro Biology.

Deoxyribose Nucleic Acid 4.1

The structure of Deoxyribose Nucleic Acid (DNA) was discovered in 1953 by James Dewey Watson.

DNA is structured such that each port on the phosphate backbone consists of one of four nucleotides: adenine, cytosine, guanine, thymine, or "a", "c", "g", "t" for short.

In all cases, adenine is bonded with thymine and cytosine is bonded with guanine.

The order of horizontal and vertical bonding matters between the two strands of DNA.

X-Ray Crystallography of DNA

Logic Gates 5.1

NAND and NOR gates are required to architect a computer system. NOT, AND, OR, XOR gates are derivable from NAND and NOR gates.

Boolean Algebra is used to manipulate logical equations.

Data Structures 5.2

Mathematical structures that hold data are called data structures. They are abstractly defined in dimensions, can be visualized, and can be defined in terms of computer architecture.

Algorithms 5.3

Mathematical structures that operate data are called algorithms.

They are abstractly defined in dimensions, can be visualized, and can be defined in terms of computer architecture.

Computational Complexity Theory 5.4

Algorithms and data structures accerate in complexity. This acceration is studied in Computational Complexity Theory.

Computer Architecture System 6.1

A computer architecture system is an underlying architecture for the architecture.

Computer architecture systems provide the application programming interfaces necessary to create operating systems.

Computer architecture systems are designed with logic and application programming interfaces.

Entropic Control 7.0

Computer systems can be used to provide for entropic control of some spaces.

Digital Design 7.1

A biological programming language is used to define input and output conditions and software creates the matching algorithm.

DNA as a String 7.2

DNA is represented by a single string of length n consisting of characters "a", "b", "c", "d" "∅" to represent the nucleotides "at", "cg", "gc", "ta", end of strand.

Programmed Modification of DNA 7.3

Map the physical actions required to splice DNA via Crispr or another method into specific computer language functions.

Some (but not all) functions are:
replace(index, nucleotide)
addleft(index, nucleotide)
addright(index, nucleotide)
remove(index, nucleotide)
verify(index)

Operate in massive parallelism to decrease total time required to modify cells.
Compile the algorithm into the most efficient physical method possible.

With Higher Specificity and Multiple Strands of DNA 7.4

The previous implementation abstracted two strands of DNA into one string. We can expand the abstraction such that we treat each strand individually.

In this case, the index is expanded into x and y coordinates where the range of x is n, the length of the strand and y is either 1 or 2, referring to either the bottom or top strand. We can add a variable z to represent multiple different strands in the case of strand breaks.

index = (x, y, z)

The nucleotides are in this case not abstracted into four characters but carry their names: "a", "c", "t", "g".
The functions operate much like the same way as before, but with higher specificity and sometimes with a need to parallel execute functions to perform certain operations.

For instance the two functions need to be executed in parallel to add cg to strand 5 right of position 2341:

addright((2341, 2, 5), c)
addright((2341, 1, 5), g)

Application Programming 8.1

Programming uses logic and application programing interfaces to create programs: logical systems designed to accomplish a purpose.

Logic is typically defined in the form of data structures and algorithms.

Application programming interfaces link to the program to the operating system.

Application Programming Interface 8.2

An application programming interface consists of an input system and an output system.

Instructions are input and feedback is recorded via output.

The feedback is read to the user, used to alter the input.

Programming Languages 8.3

Programming languages abstract logic into linguistic form.

Operating System 9.1

An operating system is an underlying architecture for the architecture.

Operating systems provide the application programming interfaces necessary to create applications.

Operating systems are designed with logic and application programming interfaces.

Book 4: CVAX Theory

Introduction 1.0

This Scientific Material is compiled by Michael Coffey.

Scientific Materials 1.1

Scientific Materials are materials that contain basic scientific information necessary to conduct research, understand a subject.

The paper before you is a Scientific Material.

Engineering 2.1

Engineering is the use of science to create technology.

Mechanical Engineering 2.2

Mechanical Engineering is the purposeful use of science to create mechanistic technology. Mechanical Engineering is a derivative of Physics, Mathematics.

Electrical Engineering 2.3

Electrical Engineering is the purposeful use of science to create electrical technology. Electrical Engineering is a derivative of Physics, Mathematics.

Aerospace Engineering 2.4

Aerospace Engineering is the purposeful use of science to create aviation technology. Aerospace Engineering is a derivative of Mechanical Engineering, Electrical Engineering.

Chemical Engineering 2.5

Chemical Engineering is the purposeful use of science to create chemical technology. Chemical Engineering is a derivative of Chemistry, Physics, Mathematics.

Computer Engineering 2.6

Computer Engineering is the purposeful use of science to create computer technology. Computer Engineering is a derivative of Electrical Engineering, Computer Science.

Material Engineering 2.7

Material Engineering is the purposeful use of science to create material technology. Material Engineering is a derivative of Chemical Engineering, Mechanical Engineering.

Biological Engineering 2.8

Biological Engineering is the purposeful use of science to create biological technology. Biological Engineering is a derivative of Computer Engineering, Biology.

Deoxyribose Nucleic Acid 3.0

The structure of Deoxyribose Nucleic Acid (DNA) was discovered in 1953 by James Dewey Watson.

DNA is structured such that each port on the phosphate backbone consists of one of four nucleotides: adenine, cytosine, guanine, thymine, or "a", "c", "g", "t" for short.

In all cases, adenine is bonded with thymine and cytosine is bonded with guanine.

The order of horizontal and vertical bonding matters between the two strands of DNA.

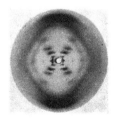

X-Ray Crystallography of DNA

DNA Genetic Expression 3.1

Deoxyribose Nucleic Acid is used to express the genetic features of an organism.

This expression occurs directly via protein creation by mRNA transcription at the cellular level. At higher levels of abstraction, multiple cells abstract to form organs, and the body of the multi-cellular organisms (i.e. humans).

DNA can be thought of as quadary code, differing from the binary code used in machine systems. Whereas machine systems have two states for a bit: "on" or "off", DNA has four states: "at" "ta" "cg" "gc".

DNA Disintegration 3.2

Deoxyribose Nucleic Acid gradually disintegrates as the organism ages.

This can be verified by comparing a DNA sample of an organism at t_1 with a DNA sample of the same organism at t_2.

The DNA sequence will be different, indicating a change in DNA, theorized to be disintegration as known by empirical observation of aging recorded in all complex multi-cellular biological organisms.

We conclude that the gradual disintegration of DNA is responsible for the aging and malignant behavior of the underlying organism, or its DNA expression, as it ages.

DNA does self repair, but self repair mechanisms cannot fully counter the entropic degradation of DNA.

CVAX Theory 3.3

CVAX Theory comprises of the theory of CAX, the theory of CVAX, and the implementation of CAX, the implementation of CVAX.

CVAX (CVAX/CAX) is a therapy developed by Michael Coffey to counter the natural entropic degradation of DNA and the subsequent aging effects of this degradation. CVAX involves CVAX and two CAX scans at two time periods, separated by at least one year, at most five to ten years.

Let t_1 be of when the organism is of a younger age and let t_2 be of when the organism is of an older age.

Scan the DNA at two points with CAX (whole genome scan) at t_1 and t_2. Correlate the differences in DNA between t_1 and t_2 then alter the DNA using CVAX such that the current DNA (t_2) is equivalent to past DNA (t_1).

It is theorized that the state change to past DNA will allow the organism to maintain the same genetic expression as when it had that DNA previously.

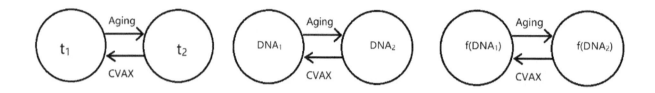

State machine model of CVAX

Implementation of CAX 4.0

CAX is implemented with DNA sequencing techniques that sequence the entire genome.

Techniques include Polymerase Chain Reaction, Effector Scan.

Implementation of CVAX 5.0

CVAX may be implemented via three methods: Viral based DNA alteration, Bacterial based DNA alteration, Effector based DNA alteration.

Implementation of CVAX via Viral based DNA alteration 5.1

When a virus infects a cell, DNA from the attacking virus enter the nucleus and modify the DNA of the host cell.

Using genetic engineering techniques, the programmed modification of DNA may be implemented via the creation of genetically engineered viruses.

Implementation of CVAX via Bacterial based DNA alteration 5.2

When a bacteriophage infects a cell, DNA from the attacking bacteriophage enter the nucleus and modify the DNA of the host cell.

Using genetic engineering techniques, the programmed modification of DNA may be implemented via the creation of genetically engineered bacteriophages.

Of note is the Crispr technique developed by Jennifer Doudna.

Implementation of CVAX via Effector based DNA alteration 5.3

The Effector is an electron transmitter. It may be used to affect the entropy of certain systems.

Effector

Effectors receive electrons, produce electromagnetic fields as a function of receiving electrons, emit electrons from a power source.

By using an effector to alter the entropy of certain biological systems, the direct or indirect modification of DNA can be achieved. This is a very advanced technique requiring advanced knowledge of entropic systems.

Artificial general intelligence paired with the effector or other entropic command and control systems may be used to implement CVAX.

Electromagnetic Circuit Model 6.0

Create a magnetic field as a function of the Effectors: $M = M_1 + M_2 + ...$
Create an electric field at a point: $E = f(M, x, y, z)$
The magnetic field is the flow of magnetons at the point.
The electric field is the flow of electrons at the point.

We can see how the Effector is a transistor by 'turning off' an Effector, say Effector 2 (M_2). By turning off Effector 2 (M_2), we 'affect' the electric field of the electromagnetic circuit. As another example, the effect of turning off Effector 2 (M_2) alters the electron flow such that electrons that would previously hit Effector 3 (M_3) no longer hit Effector 3, causing Effector 3 (M_3) to turn off, setting a chain reaction.

The logic gates NAND and NOR are derivable from the Electromagnetic Circuit Model equations via the use of Effectors that receive electrons, produce magnetic fields as a function of receiving electrons, emit electrons. In the following cases, the electrons emitted from the first Effector are ignored.

Let's create a NAND gate. We have an electric field that feeds two electrons to two Effectors, generating a stable magnetic field which allows for the electric field from the second Effector to feed into thin air, that is, not the third Effector.

By blocking or altering the electron from entering the first or second Effector, the magnetic field is altered such that the electric field no longer allows for the electric field from the second Effector to feed into thin air, and it now feeds into the third Effector.

Therefore, we have a NAND gate.

Let's create a NOR gate. We have an electric field that feeds two electrons to two Effectors, generating a stable magnetic field which allows for the electric field from the second Effector to feed into thin air, that is, not the third Effector.

For a NOR gate, removing one electron input to either Effector one or two does not significantly affect the output magnetic and electric field from its initial state, that is, the electric field from the second Effector will feed into thin air, not the third Effector.

If both electron inputs are removed and no electrons feed into Effectors one and two, Effectors one and two will turn off such that the electric field from Effector two will feed into the third Effector.

Therefore, we have a NOR gate.